RUTH

HOPE FOR THE MARGINALIZED

Other studies in the Not Your Average Bible Study series

Psalms

Jonah

Malachi

Sermon on the Mount

Ephesians

Colossians

Hebrews

James

1 Peter

2 Peter and Jude

1–3 John

For updates on this series, visit lexhampress.com/nyab

RUTH

HOPE FOR THE MARGINALIZED

NOT YOUR AVERAGE BIBLE STUDY

MILES CUSTIS

Ruth: Hope for the Marginalized
Not Your Average Bible Study

Copyright 2014 Lexham Press

Lexham Press, 1313 Commercial St., Bellingham, WA 98225
LexhamPress.com

ISBN 978-1-57-799552-4

Editor-in-Chief: John D. Barry
Managing Editor: Rebecca Van Noord
Assistant Editors: Elizabeth Vince, Joel Wilcox, Jessi Strong
Cover Design: Christine Gerhart
Typesetting: projectluz.com

CONTENTS

HOW TO USE THIS RESOURCE

Not Your Average Bible Study is a series of in-depth Bible studies that can be used for individual or group study. Depending on your individual needs or your group pace, you may opt to cover one lesson a week or more.

Each lesson prompts you to dig deep into the Word—as such, we recommend you use your preferred translation with this study. The author used his own translation, but included quotations from the English Standard Version. Whatever Bible version you use, please be sure you leave ample time to get into the Bible itself.

To assist you, we recommend using the Faithlife Study Bible, which contains notes written by Miles Custis and is also edited by John D. Barry. You can download this digital resource for free for your tablet, phone, personal computer, or use it online. Go to FaithlifeBible.com to learn more.

May God bless you in the study of His Word.

INTRODUCTION

The Old Testament is full of stories about God using great leaders like David and Moses. But God is not concerned only with people of power or status. Ruth and Naomi were women who had neither power nor position: Both were widows, and one was a foreigner. Although their circumstances were dire and they had little hope for the future, God used the events of their lives to pave the way for the Savior of humanity.

PART I: FOR A GREATER PURPOSE

RUTH 1–2

It's in our victories that we most often see God working. His blessings and gifts are evidence of His love. But when we are in the midst of suffering, can we see God's hand? In these next eight lessons, we'll learn that God's promises are not dependent on our circumstances. We'll see how God uses the lives of ordinary people to achieve His extraordinary purposes.

GOD'S HAND IN HISTORY

Pray that God would give you understanding as you begin to study the book of Ruth.

Read the entire book of Ruth aloud in one sitting.

This book was read aloud in synagogues during the Jewish feast of Shavuot (or Pentecost), which celebrated the wheat harvest. The book tells just one story, and it's important to take in the complete story at once. Reading aloud also allows us to engage the text with more than one sense.

Underline or highlight the words spoken by each character. As you study the biblical narrative, you can learn about the main characters by paying attention to how they are portrayed. How does the author portray Naomi, Ruth and Boaz? How do other characters describe these individuals?

_____

_____

_____

_____

_____

Notice how often each character speaks. How does their speech convey their value? What does each character say about God?

_____

_____

_____

_____

_____

The book of Ruth closes with a genealogy pointing to David and eventually to Jesus (see Matt 1:1-17). God uses the seemingly minor events of this story—events that affect only a few people—as part of His larger plan to bring salvation to the world. What seemingly insignificant events in your life has God used to achieve a greater purpose?

_____

_____

_____

_____

FAMINE AND TRAGEDY

Pray that the Holy Spirit would show you how God uses all things for His purpose.

Read Ruth 1:1–22. Reflect on Ruth 1:1–5.

This section provides the setting of the story and sets up the primary challenge facing the main characters. The events of this story occur "in the days when the judges ruled" (1:1). Read Judges 17–21. Note the repeated refrain that "each one did what was right in his own eyes" (Judg 17:6; 21:25). How does understanding this background affect your view of the characters?

_____

_____

_____

_____

God had forbidden the Israelites from marrying Canaanites because doing so would cause the Israelites to follow Canaanite gods instead of Yahweh (Deut 7:3–4). Although the Israelites were not prohibited from marrying Moabite women (see the list in Deut 7:1), a prior instance where Israelites and Moabites intermarried had ended in idolatry and disaster (see Num 25:1–5). Do you think it was wrong for Mahlon and Kilion to marry Orpah and Ruth? Why or why not?

_____

_____

_____

_____

_____

Naomi and her family travel to Moab because of a famine. The Old Testament includes several other accounts of people relocating due to famine (Gen 12:10–20; 26:1–33; 42:1–47:12). Naomi's family hopes to find a fresh start in Moab, but instead they find more tragedy. By the end of this section, Naomi has lost her husband as well as her sons, and she is living in Moab as a foreigner. How does God use this tragedy for good?

_____

_____

_____

Why do you think God uses negative circumstances to fulfill His purposes? Are there times in your life when God has used tragedy for a greater purpose?

_____

_____

_____

A TOUGH DECISION

Pray that God would help you trust in His unfailing love.

Read Ruth 1:1–22. Reflect on Ruth 1:6–14.

Why do you think Naomi encourages Orpah and Ruth to return home? Is she acting out of kindness, or is she hoping to free herself from the burden of them?

_____

_____

_____

Why do you think Naomi's daughters-in-law wanted to remain with her? Ruth is later commended for her decision to remain with Naomi (2:11–12), but Orpah is never condemned for returning home. Was her decision wrong? What do Orpah and Ruth's decisions show us about their character?

_____

_____

_____

It seems that Naomi has given up on God's love for her (1:12), but she hopes that He will show kindness to Orpah and Ruth. The word she uses for "kindness" refers to God's unfailing, covenantal love. God ends up showing His love to Naomi by providing an heir for her through Ruth (2:20; 4:14–15). Where else in the Bible does God display His faithful love despite human doubt? What does this say about God's unfailing love?

_____

_____

_____

In times of difficulty, how can you remember that God's love is unfailing?

_____

_____

_____

LOYALTY

Pray that the Holy Spirit would make you as committed to God as Ruth was to Naomi.

Read Ruth 1:1–22. Reflect on Ruth 1:15–18.

Ruth's first speech is an eloquent display of loyalty. It would have been much easier for Ruth to return home and start fresh. What do you think motivated her to stay with Naomi? Read 1:17. What does this passage demonstrate about Ruth's commitment to Naomi?

_____

_____

_____

Who or what are you committed to in your life? Are you as committed to God as Ruth was to Naomi?

_____

_____

_____

By staying with Naomi, Ruth distances herself from Chemosh, the god of Moab (see 1 Kgs 11:7) and aligns herself with Yahweh. Naomi had just claimed that "the hand of Yahweh has gone out against me" (Ruth 1:13), making Ruth's commitment to Yahweh all the more impressive. How does Ruth's loyalty to Naomi exemplify God's loyalty to His people?

_____

_____

_____

Read Leviticus 26:11–13, Jeremiah 32:37–41, and Ezekiel 11:17–20. How do the statements in these passages demonstrate God's covenant loyalty?

_____

_____

_____

How should God's promises of loyalty affect our lives (see 2 Cor 6:14–7:1)?

_____

_____

_____

RETURNING EMPTY

Pray that God would reveal His sovereignty and help you trust Him in times of trial.

Read Ruth 1:1–22. Reflect on Ruth 1:19–22.

The narrative glosses over what must have been a difficult journey back to Bethlehem. It focuses instead on how the women of Bethlehem react to Naomi's return and how Naomi herself reacts. The women of Bethlehem are unsure if the woman returning is actually Naomi. How do you think she has changed? Naomi instructs everyone to call her Mara, meaning "bitter." Is this an appropriate response to her circumstances?

_____

_____

_____

_____

_____

How do you respond to difficult circumstances? How *should* you respond (see Phil 4:4–7)?

_____

_____

_____

_____

_____

_____

Naomi attributes her misfortune to God. Her speech here can be compared to Job's speeches. She uses a name for God—Shaddai (or "Almighty")—found throughout the book of Job. Like Job, she has lost her family and security. And like Job, she feels that God has caused her to suffer and has now turned against her (Job 6:4; 16:9). Is there any truth in Naomi's statement? What about it is false?

_____

_____

_____

Read God's response to Job's complaints (Job 38:1–41:34). What does God emphasize in His speeches? How can His response comfort those who are experiencing trials? How can remembering God's ultimate plan for Naomi and Ruth help you as you go through trials?

_____

_____

_____

A "CHANCE" MEETING

Pray that God would give you a heart for others.

Read Ruth 1:1–2:23. Reflect on Ruth 2:1–7.

In chapter 2, Ruth volunteers to provide for Naomi and herself by asking Naomi for permission to glean grain. What does this say about Ruth's character?

_____

_____

_____

_____

Compare Ruth's attitude here with Naomi's attitude in 1:20–21. What does each woman's attitude reveal about her personality?

_____

_____

_____

_____

The narrator describes Ruth's arrival at Boaz's field as happening "by chance." Naomi later attributes this "chance" encounter to God's provision. How do you look at the circumstances of your own life?

_____

_____

_____

_____

How might God be using people in your life to challenge and encourage you to live for Him? How might God be using you in their lives?

_____

_____

_____

Boaz is introduced in 2:1 as "a prominent rich man." This phrase can also be translated as "a mighty man of valor." It could refer to Boaz's character as well as his wealth. How does Boaz's interaction with his servants display his character?

_____

_____

_____

The ancient Israelites had laws about providing for the poor. Read Leviticus 19:9–10, 23:22 and Deuteronomy 24:19–22. What do these laws say about the character of God? What are their implications for believers today? In what ways could you better display God's concern for the poor?

_____

_____

_____

GOD'S PROVISION

Pray that the Lord would give you shelter in the shadow of His wings.

Read Ruth 2:1–2:23. Reflect on Ruth 2:8–16.

In this section, Boaz generously provides for Ruth. He ensures her protection and gives her full access to his fields. He even instructs his servants to leave bundles of grain for her. What does Boaz's treatment of Ruth say about his character? What does it say about hers?

_____

_____

_____

Compare Boaz's description of Ruth ("my daughter," 2:8) with his servants' description of her ("a Moabite girl," 2:6); also compare Ruth's description of herself ("a foreigner," 2:10). Why does Boaz view Ruth differently than those around her do?

_____

_____

_____

In 2:12, Boaz blesses Ruth and prays that God will reward her work. This is the second blessing bestowed on Ruth (see 1:8–9). How are the blessings similar? What do they say about God's concern for Ruth?

_____

_____

_____

_____

Boaz blesses Ruth for taking refuge under God's wings (2:12). This is a common image in the Old Testament: Read Psalms 36, 57, 61 and 91. What characteristics of God do these psalms display? What are the benefits of taking refuge in the shadow of God's wings?

_____

_____

_____

THE REDEEMER REVEALED

Pray that God would give you a greater understanding of His love through the redemptive work of Christ.

Read Ruth 2:1–2:23. Reflect on Ruth 2:17–23.

When Ruth mentions Boaz, Naomi immediately sees the implications: Boaz is related to Naomi's deceased husband and can act as a kinsman-redeemer for them. For background on the responsibilities of a kinsman-redeemer and Levirate marriage, read Leviticus 25:23–28, 47–49 and Deuteronomy 25:5–10.

Naomi's speech in Ruth 2:20 is almost the complete opposite of her earlier claims. She had previously claimed that God had forsaken her (see 1:13, 20–21), but now she claims that God's loyal love does not forsake the living or the dead. Naomi doubted God's love when things were difficult and let her experiences affect her understanding of His faithfulness. Despite this, God remained faithful. How do you understand God's faithfulness during struggles? What can you do to ensure that your view of God's love isn't dependent on your circumstances?

_____

_____

_____

Naomi describes Boaz using the Hebrew word *go'el*, or "redeemer." This term is often used to describe God. Read Isaiah 43:14–21, 44:6–8 and Job 19:25–29. How do the descriptions of God in these passages help you understand Him as your redeemer?

_____

_____

_____

_____

Ultimately, God redeemed the world through the death and resurrection of His Son (see Rom 3:24; Eph 1:6). How does God's greater plan of redemption give you a better understanding of His faithfulness (see 2 Cor 1:18–22; Heb 10:23–25)?

_____

_____

_____

CONCLUSION

God's love and faithfulness aren't sporadic. Like Naomi, we may experience times when it is difficult to see His work. But He is present during trial and triumph. The problem is our perception, not His presence. We can confidently say that God's "loyal love has not forsaken the living or the dead" (Ruth 2:20). May you remember God's loyalty in the hard times. May you gladly offer that loyalty back to Him. And may you recognize when His purpose is being accomplished in your life.

RUTH 3–4

God's powerful acts captivate us. We're drawn to biblical stories that display His power to Israel and the surrounding nations, such as the deliverance of His people from Egyptian captivity or His acts of intercession on the battlefield (Judg 7; 2 Kgs 18–19). But sometimes His power is displayed in smaller, subtler ways.

In the story of Ruth, God moves through the characters' lives and circumstances to demonstrate His faithfulness. We see this in Ruth's devotion to her mother-in-law and Boaz's sacrificial generosity. Not only do their actions model godly behavior, but they also show how faithfully God provided for Naomi and Ruth. In the next eight lessons, we'll see how God, in providing for two women who had no hope, advanced His plan of salvation.

SEEING GOD

Pray that God would help you understand Him better as you study His word.

Read the entire book of Ruth aloud.

Because this book tells one complete story, it's helpful to read it in one sitting. When you read aloud, you can add inflection or emotion to the dialogue, which will help you understand and relate to each character's situation.

Paying attention to the progression of events when studying biblical narrative helps us recognize the themes in a story. Notice how the events in the book of Ruth unfold. How is God present through tragedies like famine or death? How does He accomplish His purposes? How do Ruth, Naomi and Boaz respond to these tragedies? How would you respond?

_____

_____

_____

Naomi, Ruth and Boaz mention God frequently. Underline each time they mention Him. How do they describe God? What do they say about Him?

_____

_____

_____

What do these statements convey about their understanding of God and their relationships with Him?

_____

_____

_____

How do you speak of God in tragedy or joyful circumstances? What needs to change for you to speak of God with words of praise and trust? (see 1:20 and 2:20).

_____

_____

_____

A BOLD PLAN

Pray that the Spirit would give you boldness to obey God's call in your life.

Read Ruth 2:1–3:5. Reflect on Ruth 3:1–5.

At the beginning of chapter 2, Ruth takes action to provide for Naomi and herself (2:2). Naomi now takes initiative as she devises a plan to find security for Ruth. Compare Naomi's attitude here to her earlier attitude (1:20–21). What accounts for this change?

_____

_____

_____

_____

In 1:9 Naomi prays that Yahweh would grant Ruth "a resting place." Originally, Naomi urged Ruth to return to her mother's home in Moab, convinced that she would find rest and security there. Now she discovers an opportunity to help Ruth find rest in Bethlehem. Have there been times in your life when you thought God would work things out one way, but He resolved them in a completely different way? How do these situations give you a better understanding of God?

_____

_____

_____

_____

Naomi's plan is bold and risky. Ruth's motivation for approaching a man at night on a threshing floor could be misunderstood (compare Hos 9:1), and neither woman knows how Boaz will react. But Ruth obeys unquestioningly. What does her obedience tell us about her relationship with Naomi?

_____

_____

_____

How does Naomi's boldness reveal her growing trust in God? Is there a situation in your life in which God is calling you to act boldly in obedience?

_____

_____

_____

A COURAGEOUS ACT

Pray that God would make you a "worthy" man or woman.

Read Ruth 3:1–13. Reflect on Ruth 3:6–13.

Ruth travels to the threshing floor—an area outside of a city where people winnow their grain, separating the grain from the plant stalk (see 1 Kgs 22:10). The events of Ruth 3 take place during the harvest, typically a time of celebration (Isa 9:3). The description of Boaz as "merry" could indicate that he is drunk or, more likely, that he is in a good mood (compare 1 Sam 25:36 and 1 Kgs 21:7). Several ambiguous terms in this section are often used as sexual innuendos (see "uncover" in Lev 18:6 or "lie down" in 2 Sam 11:4). The uncertainty of these terms heightens the tension of Ruth's actions.

When Ruth finally speaks to Boaz, she identifies herself as "your servant." Compare this with her self-description in Ruth 2:10 and 2:13. How does Boaz address Ruth (2:8; 3:11)? How do you think Boaz's view of Ruth affects how Ruth views herself?

_____

_____

_____

_____

Read Galatians 4:3–7. How does Paul's description of how God views you affect how you view yourself?

_____

_____

_____

_____

Ruth asks Boaz to spread his garment over her—a play on words since the Hebrew word for "garment" literally means "wings." Earlier, Boaz had prayed that God would reward Ruth for seeking refuge under His wings (Ruth 2:12). Now he has an opportunity to fulfill that prayer. Boaz responds by blessing Ruth and reassuring her.

Note Boaz's description of Ruth's reputation in 3:11. This phrase—"worthy woman"—is used in Proverbs 31:10 to describe the ideal woman. Read Proverbs 31:10-31. Compare the description of the "worthy woman" there with how Ruth is described. What does it mean to be worthy?

_____

_____

_____

A NEW IDENTITY

Pray that the Lord would give you patience as you await His timing.

Read Ruth 3:1–18. Reflect on Ruth 3:14–18.

In chapter 2, Boaz generously provides for Ruth and Naomi. Here we witness his ongoing benevolence as he gives Ruth barley to bring home to Naomi (3:15). Why do you think Boaz shows such generosity to Ruth and Naomi? How would his actions have comforted Ruth and Naomi as they waited to hear from him?

_____

_____

_____

When Ruth returns, Naomi literally asks her, "Who are you, my daughter?" (3:16). This is the third time that someone has asked about Ruth's identity (see 2:5 and 3:9). How do these questions emphasize the progression of Ruth's identity—from foreign widow to ancestor of King David? What does this emphasis say about how God views us?

_____

_____

_____

The chapter ends with dramatic tension as Naomi and Ruth wait to hear from Boaz. Naomi says that Boaz "will not rest but will settle the matter today" (3:18). What does Naomi's faith in Boaz tell us about him? What does it tell us about Naomi?

_____

_____

_____

Think of a situation in which you had to wait for highly anticipated news. What was your attitude while you waited? How can you learn to trust God with the details of your life?

REDEMPTION

Pray that God would teach you to love others sacrificially.

Read Ruth 3:1–4:6. Reflect on Ruth 4:1–6.

Boaz is not Ruth's closest relative and therefore does not have the first right of redemption. He asks the closer relative about redeeming Naomi's land along with Ruth. This relative has the option of purchasing Naomi's land and taking Ruth as a wife. If he decides not to, then the right will be passed to Boaz. (For background on the redemption of property, read Lev 25:23–28. For an example of someone redeeming property, read Jer 32:6–15.)

Initially the closer relative agrees to redeem the land. However, when Boaz adds the stipulation that he must also accept Ruth, "to perpetuate the name of the dead in his inheritance," the relative changes his mind. Read Deuteronomy 25:5–10. The purpose of having the closest relative marry a widow—a legal process known as Levirate marriage—was to provide children to support the widow and to preserve the name and inheritance of her deceased husband.

By agreeing to a Levirate marriage, redeeming Ruth along with the land, the closer relative would have to split his estate between his own descendants and any offspring he might have with Ruth (who would carry on the line of Elimelech). What does his decision say about his character? Is he acting selfishly or merely looking out for any children he may already have?

_____

_____

_____

_____

_____

_____

The closer relative's decision to forego his right of redemption opens the way for Boaz to redeem Ruth. What does Boaz's willingness to redeem Ruth and perpetuate the name of Ruth's deceased husband show us about his values? How does this event compare with the portrayal of Boaz throughout the book (see Ruth 2:1, 4, 14–16; 3:15–17)?

_____

_____

_____

What steps do you need to take to ensure you emulate Boaz's character?

_____

_____

_____

GOD'S PROVISION

Pray that you would be able to see how God is working in your life.

Read Ruth 4:1–12. Reflect on Ruth 4:7–12.

Boaz officially redeems Ruth before the elders and all the people. The narrator notes that Boaz and the closer relative follow "the custom in former times" (4:7). Read Deuteronomy 25:5–10. How does the legal procedure that Boaz and the closer relative follow differ from the one described in Deuteronomy? Does Ruth express the disgrace emphasized in Deuteronomy (see Deut 25:9–10)?

_____

_____

_____

_____

After Boaz expresses his intention to redeem Ruth and continue the line of Elimelech, the people pronounce a blessing on Ruth. They pray that God will make her like Rachel and Leah, who were considered the mothers of Israel (Ruth 4:11; see Gen 25:23–26). Ruth is no longer "the Moabite"; she is now likened to the revered matriarchs of Israel. Consider the progression of events that brings Ruth from a widow in Moab to this point in her life. What decisions did Ruth, Naomi and Boaz make that contributed to this change? How is God's hand evident in the course of events?

_____

_____

_____

_____

_____

The people also pray that the house of Boaz and Ruth will be like that of Perez, the son of Judah and Tamar (Ruth 4:12). Perez is also the starting point of the genealogy in 4:18–22. Read Genesis 38:1–30. What are some similarities between Tamar's story and Ruth's? What are some differences? How is God's hand evident in Tamar's story?

_____

_____

_____

How have you seen evidence of God's work in your life? How can you be quick to praise Him for this?

_____

_____

_____

THE COMMUNITY ASPECT

Pray that people would praise God for His work in your life.

Read Ruth 4:1–17. Reflect on Ruth 4:13–17.

God enables Ruth and Boaz to conceive, suggesting that Ruth may have been previously barren (note that she and Mahlon were married for about 10 years without having children; see 1:4). This is only the second time that the narrator has mentioned God acting (the other time is 1:6). Both times, God acts to provide for His people. Read Naomi's descriptions of God in 1:13 and 1:20–21. How are His actions different than the actions Naomi attributes to Him?

_____

_____

_____

_____

_____

Have you ever questioned God in difficult times? How can Ruth and Naomi's story encourage you to remain faithful through struggles?

_____

_____

_____

_____

_____

_____

The events in the book of Ruth take place in the lives of two women, yet they also affect the community. Note how God's provision for Naomi and Ruth causes the women of the community to bless God. Compare their statements here to their reaction to Naomi's return from Moab (see 1:19–21). Have there been times when God's work in your life caused others to praise Him? If not, how can you speak intentionally about God's work in your life? Are there situations in which you have praised God for working in the lives of others? How can you be more reflective of God's work in the lives of others?

_____

_____

_____

The women bless God for providing a redeemer for Naomi (4:14). They proclaim that Ruth is more valuable to Naomi than seven sons (4:15). Seven symbolizes completeness (see also Gen 2:2–3; Job 1:2). In biblical times, sons were valued because they could protect and provide for their mothers. In what ways was Ruth valuable to Naomi? How can you be valuable to others?

_____

_____

_____

THE BIGGER PICTURE

Pray that the Lord would show you his concern for your life.

Read Ruth 4:1–22. Reflect on Ruth 4:18–22.

The book of Ruth begins with a statement that places it within its historical context ("In the days when the judges ruled"; 1:1). It concludes with a genealogy that connects the story to events in Israel's history. This genealogy also reveals the broader implications of the events in the book of Ruth.

Ruth and Boaz's child would become the grandfather of David, the great king of Israel. The women's prayer that the child's "name be renowned in Israel" (4:14) is fulfilled beyond what they could have expected. Have you ever prayed for something and seen God provide far more than you had anticipated?

_____

_____

_____

_____

Matthew mentions Ruth in the genealogy of Jesus. Read Matthew 1:1–17. What other women are mentioned in this genealogy? What are some similarities among these women? What does their inclusion in Jesus' genealogy convey about what is important to God?

_____

_____

_____

_____

_____

The book of Ruth shows God's concern for individual lives and points to His plan of salvation. How do you understand God's care and concern for you as an individual?

_____

_____

_____

Write down your prayers or your requests to God. How does He answer them? How is He working in your life, whether He answers your prayers in the affirmative or negative?

_____

_____

_____

How has God revealed His plan of salvation in your life?

_____

_____

_____

CONCLUSION

God is concerned about the day-to-day struggles of ordinary people as much as He is with those who are part of big picture events. In the book of Ruth, He works through everyday circumstances and faithfully provides for two seemingly ordinary women—Naomi and Ruth. Yet by arranging rest for Ruth and Naomi, He also paves the way for His extraordinary plan of salvation—ultimate rest through the work of Jesus Christ. God cares about your struggles and difficulties today just as much as He cared about Naomi and Ruth's. May you feel God's hand in all aspects of your life, and may your actions display His love to others.

Make Your Bible Study Even Better

Get 30% off Bible Study Magazine.

Subscribe today!